Propolis for a Fractured World

propolis | ˈpräpələs | noun

a red or brown resinous substance collected by honeybees from tree buds, used by them to fill crevices and to seal and varnish honeycombs. It is also said to have many medicinal and healing properties.

little prayer
Danez Smith

let ruin end here
let him find honey
where there was once a slaughter
let him enter the lion's cage
& find a field of lilacs

let this be the healing
& if not   let it be
the end of ruin

Also by Greg Stidham:

Iced Tea Poetry
(Silver Bow Publishing 2023)

Blessings and Sudden Intimacies
(PathBinder Publishers, 2021)

Dear Friends
(PathBinder Publishers, 2021)

Doctoring in Nicaragua
(Finishing Line Press, 2021)

Propolis
for a
Fractured World

by

Greg Stidham

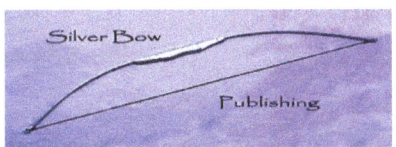

720 Sixth Street, Box # 5
New Westminster, BC
CANADA V3L 3C5

Title: Propolis for a Fractured World
Author: Greg Stidham
Cover Art: "Flight of the Bumblebee" painting by Candice James
Layout and Editing: Candice James
© 2024 Silver Bow Publishing

All rights reserved including the right to reproduce or translate this book or any portions thereof, in any form except for the use of short passages for review purposes, no part of this book may be reproduced, in part or in whole, or transmitted in any form or by any means, electronically or mechanically, including photocopying, recording, or any information or storage retrieval system without prior permission in writing from the publisher or a license from the Canadian Copyright Collective Agency (Access Copyright)

Library and Archives Canada Cataloguing in Publication

Title: Propolis for a fractured world / by Greg Stidham.
Names: Stidham, Greg, author.
Identifiers: Canadiana (print) 20240412931 | Canadiana (ebook) 20240414977 | ISBN 9781774033104
   (softcover) | ISBN 9781774033111 (ebook)
Subjects: LCGFT: Poetry.
Classification: LCC PS8637.T535 P76 2024 | DDC C811/.6—dc23

Propolis for a Fractured World

I humbly dedicate this collection of poems to the great poet, Ted Kooser, who has been an inspiration to me through his poetry for many years. He has, for more than half a century, been the inspiration to the opening of the eyes and the hearts of many tens of thousands more who have been lucky to happen across his work.

Propolis for a Fractured World

INTRODUCTION

In 2016 or so I became a beekeeper. I knew almost nothing about keeping bees, so I relied on the cumulative knowledge of my wife, who'd kept bees several decades ago, in her twenties. We bought a new type of hive, called a "Flow Hive™. It was a revolutionary design which vastly simplified the gathering of honey, reduced the amount of equipment needed, and made it possible to tend to many beekeeping tasks without ever disturbing the bees, without their noticing our presence.

But, we were not legal. The town where we live has city regulations that prohibit the keeping of "livestock" in city limits. And, yes, bees are considered livestock; but chickens are not. Please, don't ask me why.

We talked to our city councilman, a neighbor, who advised us to be quiet, be sure our neighbors were ok with it, and don't tell him anything further <*wink wink*>. So, we have been stealth beekeepers of one hive, under the radar, for several years. We did consult with our neighbors, almost all of whom are avid gardeners and they were thrilled. And even more thrilled when we shared the riches of their robustly flourishing gardens, and they received our fresh and pure honey.

Thus began my many years of fascination—borderline obsession—with bees, and my deep affection for them. We joined the local beekeepers' guild, made some friends, and garnered a great deal of advice—some of it confusing, even conflicting. And as we embarked on *"parenting"* our first colony, I read everything and watched every YouTube video I could get my hands on. Soon I began to realize the more I learned about bees, the more there was to learn.

Bees are complex creatures. Social creatures. Efficient creatures. They communicate in many ways, some of which we know, and many of which we do not understand. Most of all, I realized we are co-inhabitants of this physical space. We all do well if we take care of each other, bees and humans alike.

I sometimes sit for an hour or more beside our hive, watching *"the girls"* come and go, industrious and dedicated. At these times, I begin to feel peace. I feel part of them and part of something larger than myself. These are times, unequivocally, of meditation.

    This short collection is my tip of the hat to my bees, and all bees. A gesture of gratitude. And a plea for their help as we navigate a physically and spiritually collapsing planet. There is a lot to be learned from bees.

~Greg Stidham

CONTENTS

1
My First Hive / 13
Picking Up Bees / 14
Flow Hive™ / 17
New-Fangled Hive / 18
Protective Garb / 21
Worker Bees / 22
Queen Bee / 23
I am a drone, / 25
Forever Marriage / 26
Feminist Commune / 27
Waggle Dance / 28
Swarming / 29
Hexagons and Octagons / 31

2
Dandelions / 35
Goodwill / 37
Bumblebee / 38
The Frantic Bumblebee / 39
The Last Bumblebee / 40
Mason Bee / 41
Yellow Jackets / 43
EpiPens / 44

3
Early Blossoms / 47
Ontario Spring / 48
Spring Equinox / 49
Abandoned Hive / 50
Lying with Honeybees / 51
Inspiration / 52
Mesmerized / 53

4

Honeybee, Early Spring / 57
Total Eclipse / 58
Poets, Bees, Beekeepers and Worms / 59
Black Bears / 60
Swarm / 61
The Real Swarm / 62

5

The Wounded Queen / 65
The Solo Honeybee / 66
Last Day / 67
Time / 68
Poetry / 69
Sunflower / 71
Mohammed Ali / 72
Afterlife / 73

Acknowledgments / 75

Propolis for a Fractured World

1

My First Hive

The first time I lifted the lid
I leaned back fearing attack
by tiny yellow dragons.
But what transfixed my gaze
was a teeming mass of alive—
moving, writhing, humming.

Bolstered by a deep breath
I stepped closer and saw
the single organic mass
was not single at all, but thousands
of individual bees,

so busy with individual tasks
they paid me no heed,
working tirelessly,
except for a curious few,
who stopped and circled my face
on their nectar-laden flight
back to the hive.

Picking Up Bees

The drive to the apiary
was sixty miles into farm country,
the nearest town home
to maybe a hundred people.

Several acres of lush greenery
perched next to a small cemetery:
no neighbors here
to complain about the bees.

Cars were lined up,
and the beekeeper breeders
busily bound the "nuc" boxes
for the bees' travels
to their "forever home."

Third in line, we waited
while a middle-aged man
loaded his temporary brood box
into his car's trunk.

When our turn came
we carefully placed
the well-taped box
in the back of our car,
headed out on the hour's drive home
in the early evening dark.

The next morning it was time
to liberate the workers
to explore their new neighborhood,
to discover the untold delights
of new spring flowers and tree pollen
that would feed their growing family.

Joyful at the relocation into their new home,
they were within hours furiously foraging,

coming and going
to and from the hive,
a sight that made me smile
during pandemic-forced isolation.

Flow Hive™

Honey flows down plastic tubes
from special frames in the hive's super—
liquid gold, swirling slowly, thickly
into Saran-covered mason jars.

So calm is the process the bees
don't notice, they're not angry,
they don't need the extra honey
and they give it up graciously,
thankful for the fondant I fed them
during the dark winter
of barely survivable cold.

New-Fangled Hive

The older, more experienced members
of the Limestone Beekeepers' Guild
made fun of us and our Flow Hive™.
"That's not real beekeeping," they said,
though they would not say why
"real beekeeping" with the need
to remove the frames and
shake the bees off, making them
angry and defensive, aggressive
was better.

They wouldn't say why buying
an expensive centrifuge
to extract honey, was better.

They were macho about their
hundred-year-old methods,
and if our Flow Hive™ was not
real beekeeping, then I guess
we are not "real" beekeepers.

I prefer my hive,
openings in the back,
frames that unlock and
free the honey to flow,
like beer from a tapped keg
in a favorite pub.

The bees continue
their business in the front,
coming and going
on their foraging voyages,
not even noticing us landlords
in the back collecting rent,
save for one or two
curious girls who
take note and turn
carefree, winking

one big eye as they fly
off to their flower fields.

Protective Garb

Like a scene from a late-50's
B sci-fi movie: the scientists don their
Haz-Mat suits, white from head to toe,
masks covering faces before they enter
the isolation room where the corpse
of an alien lies after being recovered
from a crashed saucer-like space vehicle,

beekeepers don their white protective overclothes
and their white-hooded bonnets
with netting falling before the face,
    like I did at first.

Over time I learned that
the honeybees are not aggressive,
rarely even curious,
so I skipped the billowy white blouse,
and later the elbow-high gloves,
until last to go was
the face-netting bonnet.

Rarely now while
sitting on my back deck
a solitary honeybee will light
on my arm, and I watch calmly
as she tickles my arm hairs,
to her as tall and thick
as prairie grasses,
and wish her well
as she then flies off
in search of nectar and pollen.

Worker Bees

1

They descend in droves
from barely discernible flight patterns
before a slow approach to their landing site,
landing gear extended,
their orange or yellow pouches
like saddlebags straddling a bicycle.
Scarcely pausing, they scramble in
to deliver their sweet spoils.

2

Hexagonal cells stacked
one on top of another,
each with six identical neighbors
in this waxy tenement,
fashioning the geometry
like an intricate Quaker quilt,
each one a resting place
for an egg the size of a white flea.

And I, a furtive voyeur,
peer through a small glass portal
and watch them, obsessed and frantic
as they clean out each room
to prepare for the next tenant.

Queen Bee

Everyone thinks
she is a prima donna.
She looks a bit different
from all the other girls;
her formal dress slightly more alluring.
Its black and yellow stripes
flowing from her shoulders,
her length highlighting her superiority.

She has her own entourage
of attendants who feed her,
clean her and groom her.
The other girls are called workers
for a reason.
They spend their lives like hotel maids,
cleaning the shared space.
Then, maintenance workers
repairing acquired defects,
using their mandible pliers
and flat-nosed trowels
to apply propolis calking.

They prepare the baby rooms,
sanitizing them with disinfectants
produced by their own bodies.
Or as sanitation workers,
they clean sewerage and dispose
of the remains of the deceased,
parading slowly to the entrance
to the dirge of their
ever-humming wings,
and the workers fly all day
to forage food for
the entire community,
and later become warriors
to defend the compound against invaders.

Propolis for a Fractured World

The queen's life expectancy far exceeds
that of the other girls, and everyone
thinks she has the easy life

    but

what they don't know
is the queen's own work.

She, like the workers,
works all day, laying eggs,
1500 a day, 200,000 in a year,
pausing I suppose to rest
at night, as the other girls do.

The worker bees
work their stingers off daily,
but for only four or five weeks,
while the queen never rests
for two or maybe three years.

The workers have their sisters
as they do their chores together,
their wings singing in unison,
while the queen has no one
as she works endlessly alone,
until she can work no more,
then the workers, thanklessly,
prepare a cell for a new queen,
who replaces her, after defeating her
in a battle she cannot possibly win.

I am a drone,

a male honeybee,
I have only one set
of chromosomes,
those of my mother,
the queen, no father.
I and my brothers
are a small minority
in this colony of females.

I don't look so different,
I'm hard to tell apart from
my sisters, and I don't even have
a stinger, and unlike
the hardworking girls
who have nearly a dozen jobs,
a dozen *raisons d'être*,
I have only one.
I am a sperm donor
and when spring arrives
I hatch and fly from the hive
in search of virgin queens,
accompanied by many
of my brothers.
We fly a distance from
our hive in search of a virgin queen
with different genetics than ours
and our mother's.

That's our purpose in life,
to find a virgin queen
seeking my sperm, and that
perhaps of a few others.

And if I am a lucky one
who scores and deposits
my sperm, I am done,
my life fulfilled,
and I fly off a bit ... and die.

Forever Marriage

They met mid-air,
the drone and the queen,
both virgins and both unsure,
but both hoping
for a forever marriage.
They court briefly,
find each other suitable,
and then they
consummate their vows.

The deed is done,
he flies off to die,
she to lay eggs,
to lead a teeming colony
for two years, using
her collected sperm,
and their forever marriage
is done in a day.

Feminist Commune

An intentional community
whose quarters are
architecturally perfect,
like their social structure.

Each cell within is a suite
sheltering a growing bee,
each cell identical to the next,
each immaculately cleaned
by the nurse bees before
they graduate on to other duties:

feeding the growing brood,
attending to the laying queen,
tidying the hive and
removing the deceased,
repairing, like contractors,
cracks in the hive's wax,
with magical propolis.

And the few who are warriors,
stand guard at the entrance
to ward off yellow jacket robbers,
even small mice when days chill.

All of these worker bees
coordinate under the benevolent
leadership of the queen,

all a rebuttal to man's
patriarchal constructions.

Waggle Dance

As a young adult
I hated the thought of dancing,
unlike a honeybee, unlike
the lucky one who hits
the floral motherlode,
comes home to the cheers
of her sisters who clear a space
in the center of the dance floor,
and like an evangelical,
a holy roller speaking in tongues
during a center stage seizure,
she begins vibrating side-to-side
while running raggedly
in figures-of-eight, all pointing
in the same direction, each 8
exactly the same duration.
After several repetitions
her sisters all know just where
and how far the blossomy bounty
will be found.
As one, they fly off
to reap this plenitude,
returning with pouches full
of pollen and nectar.
She's done her job.

I know I danced once,
a dance at my first wedding,
but a dance I can't remember,
just as this dancing bee
will soon forget her
once-in-a lifetime
waggle dance.

Swarming

No warning this time,
no bearding,
no increased activity
at the hive's entrance,
just a neighbor's text,
"Are your bees swarming?"
and we aborted running errands
to return home,
pulled into the driveway,
and there they were,
clustered in our neighbor's tree,

thirty feet up in a conical ball
half again the size of a basketball
clinging tightly together,

ten or fifteen thousand, except
for a few stragglers
too heavy with honey
to go off house hunting.

The fugitives wait for the scouts
to start their search for fresh sites
before their final big move.

Disappointing to the keeper,
this is what they are supposed to do,
this is how they preserve their species.

Now with a hive half-depleted,
the keeper is chagrined,
but take cheer my friend,
they do what they are meant to do,
and they are able to
because of good stewarding,
emerging from winter
healthy and strong.

Hexagons And Octagons

Hexagon: the shape of the small cells
in my first beehive, where the queen
backs her rear into each cell,
a delivery truck with eggs
but without the "beep-beep-beep,"
fifteen hundred times a day,
and where the workers
bring their pollen and nectar
to 150,000 cells to feed
the growing brood.

Octagon: the red sign
outside my kitchen window,
poised at the end of our quiet street,
the street where Wednesday mornings
the recycling pick-up trucks
wake me, barely after light,
with their "beep-beep-beep."

2

Dandelions

My father was fastidious
about our lawn, the type of grass,
the seeding and later
the sodding–Zoysia, Bermuda.

He pushed the two-wheeled
fertilizer spreader,
until I was old enough—
a chore for my allowance.

Dandelions were a curse
of biblical proportions,
to be eradicated as soon
as spotted, by smelly
petroleum poisons squirted
from a tank with a pressure handle.

Today, older than my father
when he died, I am
an illegal urban beekeeper,
and I've learned to love dandelions,
embrace these first spring donors
of pollen and nectar,
to feel their tickle
between my bared toes.
These same plants are those
my father's mother boiled
to make "dandelion greens,"
to garnish the ham
and black-eyed peas.

I am now like I was
as a boy with questions:
why poison wildflowers,
to burn out a lawn for Zoysia sod,
why kill these wildflowers

loved by bees, and loved by my toes,
toes that slowly pace
the ungainly front yard
we call our lawn,
and I sign petitions to ban Round-Up
and to call Monsanto to account,
and I pray to keep my bees safe.

Goodwill

The honeybees hover
over patches of color
in the backyard garden,
selectively descending

on one flower or another,
choosing one, finishing
and flitting to the next,
oblivious to the bumblebee

foraging the flower
right next door,
each going about
her separate business.

If you know what to seek
you will also see mason bees,
maybe leafcutters, and looking
carefully the diminutive sweat bees.

They all arduously do their work
in respectful solitude somehow
never straying one into
the domain of another.

They work in peaceful harmony,
no fighting over one flower,
no defensive posturing,
no colonial invasions.

I sit and watch them for hours,
puzzling at their cordial coexistence,
wondering why we can't live peacefully
as they so easily do.

Bumblebee

A white-haired woman in her fifties
walks past my front-yard wooden bench,
with her daughter, or perhaps grand-child.

Their animated hands converse excitedly,
the girl behind mumbling
to make her signing right.

A furry-jacketed bumblebee
touches the tops
of grass blades awaiting mowing—
to her the size of treetops,
she, moving one to the next,
as oblivious to me, as were
the woman and the child.

The Frantic Bumblebee

This newly erected, screened gazebo tent,
meant to deter menacing mosquitos
and other merciless invaders,
mayflies early on, yellowjackets later,
but not our honeybees who would be here
only if they got trapped while nectar-foraging.

And also not the docile bumblebee,
like the one today who found herself
ensnared within this house of mirrors,
screens that don't obscure the infinite,
the beautiful universe without.

She was frantic, flying non-stop,
crashing into barriers she couldn't see,
unperturbed by the keyboard clacking
on the outdoor table below.

Flying frenetically, non-stop,
seeking a way to escape her nightmare,
until she was exhausted,
unused to constant flight
without the respite of finding one
after another dusty colorful flower,
and she paused,
poised on a metal frame
of this canvas structure.

Then, like magic,
the side screen was lifted,
exposing the world as she knew it,
and she darted out into the waning sunlight,
and back to her earthen hive home.

The Last Bumble Bee

The bumble bee colony in our insulation
has died its natural death,
signaled by the cold of late autumn.
The workers are gone,
and the queens fly in search of holes
in the soon-to-be frozen earth.
There they will doze until drawn out
by warming days of spring
beckoning the building of another nest,
and then the task of laying eggs.

But one queen has become trapped
inside our small kitchen where
she roars from wall to window,
sounding like a small aircraft,
puzzled at what prevents her
darting out into the sunshine
she so plainly sees.

Deftly maneuvering a paper cup
and a piece of stiff paper
we catch her, carry her
to the back door, and like
dancing in prayer to the sunshine,
we lift our arms, and set her free.

Mason Bee

Little known first cousins of honeybees,
mason bees are the black sheep in the family.
They live their lives in solitude,
follow no social rules,
build no hives,
don't strive against odds
to survive winter,
like their cousins.

Masons have no respect for authority,
no queen to serve, worship,
feed and clean, no need
to nurture an egg
into a new queen
to replace one who is sickly
or aging and less fertile.

The mason may lay
twenty eggs in a lifetime,
unlike her industrious cousin's
200,000 in a season.

Like her cousin she relies
on pollen and nectar for her offspring,
but she alone collects from the flowers,
while her Queen cousin has 30,000 daughters
collecting for the entire colony.

Her drabness boosts
the famous beauty of her cousin
always dressed in two-tone stripes,
usually tastefully contrasting
yellow and black, but the mason's colors
are dull, greys or drab tan,
though rarely a metallic green.

In one week the eggs hatch,

then more weeks for the larvae
to knit new shawls
and wrap themselves in a cocoon
for winter hibernation,
emerging in the next season.

Her nest is simple and small,
one she will never occupy,
but where she will lay her eggs
in a line, six at a time,
in a dark and lonely tube,
a dark and lonely time machine.

There is much to admire
about the honeybee queen,
who will live her life
of two or three years,
served by her generations
of adoring daughters,

but there is also much
to admire about the black sheep
mason bee, who will have
a couple dozen daughters,
living her own life
in one season, marching
to her own drummer,
and then die satisfied,
before winter,
knowing her daughters
will emerge in a few months
when the weather
again turns warm.

Yellow Jackets

Six years old, the boy stops
kicking the ball in the short
newly-mowed grass
in the backyard near the house,
and he watches with awe
and curiosity his father pushing
the new gas-powered mower
at the rear of the deep back yard.

He wandered toward the back
with curiosity when suddenly,
his father howled, stopping the mower,
and began running toward the house,
followed by a hoard of black creatures,
who turned also on the boy,
who was soon attacked
by the hot pinpricks of stings;
bee stings his mother told him,
as she rubbed baking soda paste
on his growing hives.

What he did not learn
for fifty years was that these
were not stings of bees;
rather stings of yellow jackets,
and for fifty years
the boy was afraid of bees,

deprived nearly a lifetime
of the tameness of honeybees,
wondering what he'd missed
as he learned about bees' society,
their ways of communicating,
their social democracy
and sharing of chores,

and then he became a beekeeper.

EpiPens

Honeybee stings are rare,
and are rarely unjustified
as they are aggressive only
when they need to be defensive,
when their hives are under attack.

And when they sting
they are annoyingly painful
for a few hours, while
the sting is fatal to the stinger.

A honeybee sting is dangerous
only if the stingee has a bee allergy,
which is also very rare.

And how many people even know
if they have a honeybee allergy?

I was surprised to learn
that my friend and bee mentor,
the Obi Wan Kenobi
of all things bees,
himself has a bee allergy
and carries an EpiPen,
just in case.

So I bought two,
out of fear of a second-grader,
perhaps walking past the wood fence,
if accidentally stung,
would discover his bee allergy.

3

Early Blossoms

Alone on a mesa,
a pink crabapple tree
embraces the wind,
its branches reaching up
and out like a menorah,
the petite blossoms a pointillist image,
mysteriously scintillating.

Up close, the shimmer buzzes:
honeybees feasting on spring's
first Rocky Mountain pollen.

Ontario Spring

In Ontario in June the kayaks appear
perched on cartops in droves,
like the children in schoolyard playgrounds,
where stickball replaces hockey.

Grandfathers rummage
through deep closets retrieving
fishing rods and reels.

But before June, in May,
straw-hatted and gloved women,
wearing short sleeves appear outdoors
in pants below the knees, small shovels in hand,
to begin the tedious tilling of the gardens
in time for the bees' awakening.

Spring Equinox

Today and tonight are equal,
one of two times this year.
The first day of spring
brings freeze tonight,
and my bees didn't survive,
drowned in their own beauty
and their own humidity,
because I failed them,
forgot the upper entrance,
the ventilation.

As a child
I forgot to change water
in my goldfish bowl.

I cried in bed that night.

Abandoned Hive

A routine visit to the honeybee hive
to be sure they were thriving,
foraging pollen and nectar.

Opening the hive and removing frames
we thought would be filled
with teeming hordes of honeybees
busily building new honeycomb,
cleaning waxy bassinets
for new eggs, but no!

No bees, no teeming—
naked frames empty of brood,
no eggs, no larvae,
just blankness, and stillness,
the only life left
that of yellow jacket robbers,
stealing old honey,
and a single wax moth,
picking at the remains
of a post-apocalyptic city,
abandoned and empty.

Lying with Honeybees

Lying back in fresh long grass,
surrounded by the scent
of fertile still-moist soil,
with dandelions littered about
like myriad small suns,
I watch downy creatures drifting
through an infinite azure sky,
and I hear the contralto buzz
around my head, as honeybees
busily tend their tasks,
foraging nectar and pollen,
blossom to hive,
oblivious to my quiet breathing
beside them.

Inspiration

Weather is a worthy inspiration:
gale-strength winds
driving rain horizontal,
lightning spears lighting skies
like the flickering
of a drive-in theater screen.

Or the soft syncopated tap
of gentle raindrops on the metal roof
of a log house in the Colorado Rockies,
seductively trance-inducing
with meandering thoughts
that demand writing down
with an old-fashioned
piston-draw fountain pen,
or a laptop computer screen.

Worthy inspiration is
a partnered couple of geese rising
from near-shore off Lake Ontario.
They ponder a flight south
as season changes, and weather too.

Another: ice on the lake in February,
a meter thick, thick enough
for racing snowmobiles,
even tents with propane fire rings
beside a small hole
cut through for ice fishing,
or even the pickerel
pulled through that hole,
passing across
from its cold underwater world
through the dark into light,
and then to the frying pan.

That is the stuff of poetry.

Mesmerized

A beginning beekeeper sits a few feet
from his first hive's entrance
during the initial spring forages,
watching bees come and go,
he, unmolested, unnoticed,
watches them descend
from twenty feet high
before braking for landing
a foot away,
gently touching down,
saddle bags full
of orange or yellow,
nectar and pollen from
the neighborhood floral bounty.

He watches, mesmerized
as though one with them.

This is the stuff of poetry.

4

Honeybee, Early Spring

Like a shy girl
at a high school dance,
she flutters at a distance unsure
before descending
to the narrow yellow petals
that have somehow
survived Monsanto and Round-Up.

She knows there's nectar there,
and pollen too, and her next generation
depend on her success,
so she dives in, inserting her proboscis,
knowing her prize will either kill her,
or nurture the next newborn generation.

Total Eclipse

The hive sits in the middle
of the Path of Totality
for next week's eclipse,
when their afternoon sun
will fall dark for two minutes.
I wonder what they will do
with their untimely nightfall,
in the midst of a day's
work foraging pollen.

Will they stop and hurry home
to bed down in a cluster
in the middle of their hive,
or will they wait it out
right where they are,
tongue stuffed into stamen
deep in the cup of a daffodil
waiting to resume work
when the sun rises again.

Poets, Bees, Beekeepers and Worms

She asked me why poets are so enamored
of beekeepers and their bees.
Why not ants, termites, worms?
And I, a beekeeping poet,
    sent her a poem
about a bee in early spring,
and another about Red Wigglers
squirming in the compost box
in our backyard, just behind the hive.

Black Bears

The log cabin sits atop a mesa,
just below the continental divide,
under the stern gaze
of 14,000-foot Mount Shavano.

At the edge of the mesa
is a steep drop into a rough ravine,
where water from rare rain
or from spring snow runoff collects,

drawing wildlife of all sorts:
deer, coyote, elk and bear.
One of our scant neighbors
keeps and tends bees,

whose honey draws bears near
and but for the barking of their
two dogs, the hive would long ago
have been raided and left

in honeyless splinters,
while sticky bear whiskers
fled like children after
bursting a bubble-gum bubble
that stains their chins.

Swarm

My neighbor called today
to say he thought our bees
were swarming, and we trusted him.
Twice before they'd swarmed,
ten or twenty thousand bees leaving the hive,
rising like smoke from a chimney,
with the sound of a helicopter landing
in their front yard.
They always nest in his tree,
high up, about twenty feet away.

This time was different,
fewer than a hundred bees,
not clustering, and the hive
seemed unchanged,
yet we'll have to check,
to see if our Queen
has abandoned us.

The Real Swarm

This one was the real one,
15,000 honeybees,
half the hive clustered
in the neighbor's tree,
the other now queenless half
probably startled by the new
spaciousness in their home.

This is reproduction at its finest,
the swarm off to find a new home
and resume growing,
the abandoned bees nurturing
a freshly hatched new queen.

5

The Wounded Queen

She was raised to be
from earliest infancy
a Queen, no choice
of her own, but of others
who chose the size of the cell
for her egg, and then
fed her the royal jelly
that changed everything.

She grew into a Queen, but
second string, she never knew
that there were others too,
other Queens-in-waiting,
and only one—the first to hatch—
would be the Queen, and
the other Queen wannabe's
would be sacrificed in a duel
with the one ordained to be
first-hatched, the others
just sacrifices
to the God of bees.

The Solo Honeybee

The sound of a honeybee
is distinct, and distinctly
different from that of a wasp
or a yellow jacket.

Honeybees are also rarely solo,
they forage together,
while wasps are more likely
solo ravagers,

which puzzled me on a spring
patio-sitting evening reading
poetry with the sun setting
behind my back.

The buzz caught my ear,
the drone clearly of a honeybee,
and I looked for her,
thinking I might be mistaken,

and then she appeared,
circling close, but non-threatening,
and I asked her why she was alone,
at this end of day hour.

She should have been home
with her sisters, readying
for darkness and a night of rest
before next day's chores.

And then I realized
this is probably her end,
the end of her five-week life.

This is what they do:
they leave their sisters,
and they die in solitude.

Last Day

She must be five weeks old,
about her life expectancy,
worked to death every single day
serving her people, finding food
and feeding them all, cleaning
until after weeks of flying, foraging,
she has nothing left, no energy,
no muscle strength to fan her wings
until now, she stumbles erratically
around on the ground
not far from the hive she served.
She falls to her side, tries to walk,
but only in circles on this,
her last day. Her job is done.

Time

My wristwatch stopped working yesterday
at 10:32, and for the rest of the day
it was 10:32, though I knew it wasn't

true when the sun started slipping
behind the pines across the road,
and my arthritic knees hurt more

than they ever do in the morning.
That started me thinking about time,
not like Einstein's time

which is scientific fact,
but humans' time which I think
may be a creation of our imagination.

They say a year in the life of a dog
is equivalent to seven human ones,
and I watch two boys playing in the street,

about six years old. For them a year
is 16% of their lives, which is why
it takes so long for Christmas to arrive.

For me a year is barely 1%,
which is why my birthday comes
and goes without notice.

And what of the honeybee
each of whose five weeks
is 15% of her life, or about
fifteen human years?

All of this makes me ponder
my remaining years which
like Einstein's pass with bluster
and the speed of light.

Poetry

The day is kind,
cool for June,
but that's Ontario:
the sun is bright, and the honeybees
fly determined from their hive
to feast on the bountiful pollen
in the many neighbors' gardens.

The thunderstorms arrive
almost unannounced, lightning first,
then thunder just seconds before
the sudden sheets of rain
pelting the streets and
the thirsty back-yard gardens
of vegetables and colorful
feeders for the bees.

Meanwhile, elsewhere,
    police brutality,
white on black violence,
    and I mourn
my country of origin,
and write poetry,
while meditating
to the hum of honeybees.

Sunflower

Our backyard garden, replete
with flowers of all varieties,
and vegetables with their flowers,
was my summer haven.

My favorite, one year,
was the solitary sunflower
stretching up to salute
its eponymous life-giver.

This was the year
of my first beehive,
and I watched the honeybees
flirting with the sunflower's many blossoms

in that garden, but
particularly I watched them
explore that solar surface
in search of pollen and nectar,

and I thank the sunflower for my bees,
and my bees for my sunflower.

Mohammed Ali

"Float like a butterfly,
sting like a bee," the famous quote
of Mohammed Ali, he meant his
delicate dance in the boxing ring,
his defiance of the rants of the champ,
George Foreman.

Butterfly dances make total sense,
but honeybees' lances make none
at all. He may have been the greatest,
but as much in civil rights as boxing,

he did not know that bees
do not sting, they're aggressive
just for show, just defensive
and never truly aggressive.

Still I love him for his courage
in his fight for civil rights,
not so much for his entourage
of celebrities and certainly not
for his knowledge of bees.

Afterlife

Promise me you'll look for me
hiding behind the stalks of dandelions
littering the lawn we agreed not to treat.

Look for me too in the rocks,
the smooth rocks lining the bank
      of Lake Ontario
just blocks from where we lived,
where small waves lightly lap.

Look for me in the hop-scotch
leaps of the children who live
just doors away, the ones
with exotic names:

Finn, Elise, Britten and Clara,
who wander home
in herds of three or four or five,
usually a parent in the lead, or not.

Look for me there
trailing along behind.
You might see me there
if you look closely.

Don't look for me in church.
I won't be there.
Look for me inside the beehive,
lowest box, near the center,
where the Queen and brood
busily are.

Look for me
in my closet,
in my cluttered office,
full of artifacts.
Look for me in your heart,

or your hippocampus,
for it is mainly there
that I can live on
and somehow be found.

ACKNOWLEDGMENTS

I would like to thank the editors or publishers for featuring certain of these poems in their publication, in current or similar form:

Silver Bow Publications, *Iced Tea Poetry*, June, 2023:
    "Worker Bees"
    "Lying with Honeybees"
    "Abandoned Hive"

Dreamers Creative Writing, Winter/Spring 2019:
    "Early Blossoms"

I would also like to thank the following: Candice James, my editor and publisher, for her excellent help and effort in preparation of this collection; my friend, Harley Gallagher, the Obi Wan Kenobi of beekeeping; and finally, my wife Pam, whose patience with my obsession with this project has been unending.

www.ingramcontent.com/pod-product-compliance
Lightning Source LLC
Chambersburg PA
CBHW060033040426
42333CB00042B/2414